D0276100

JN 2122552

COUNTY
LIBRARY

START-UP HISTORY

HOMES

Stewart Ross

Evans

Evans Brothers Limited

Published by Evans Brothers Limited
2A Portman Mansions
Chiltern Street
London W1U 6NR

Reprinted 2006

Produced for Evans Brothers Limited by
White-Thomson Publishing Ltd.
2/3 St Andrew's Place
Lewes, East Sussex BN7 1UP

Printed in China by WKT Co. Ltd.

Editor: Anna Lee
Consultant: Norah Granger
Designer: Tessa Barwick

Cover (centre): a Victorian sitting room at York
 Castle Museum.
Cover (top left): Victorian chimney pots.
Cover (top right): a 1940s cooker.

The right of Stewart Ross to be identified as the author of
this work has been asserted by him in accordance with the
Copyright, Designs and Patents Act 1988.

© Evans Brothers Limited 2002

All rights reserved. No part of this publication may be
reproduced, stored in a retrieval system or transmitted in
any form, or by any means, electronic, mechanical,
photocopying, recording or otherwise, without the prior
permission of Evans Brothers Limited.

British Library Cataloguing in Publication Data

Ross, Stewart
  Homes. - (Start-up history)
  1.Dwellings - History - Juvenile literature
  2.Housing - History - Juvenile literature
  I.Title
  640.9

ISBN: 0 237 52407 4
13 - digit ISBN (from 1 Jan 2007) 978 0 237 52407 4

Acknowledgements: The publishers would like to thank
Richard Stansfield of York Castle Museum for his assistance
with this book, and Smith Bros. of Osbaldwick for their
kind permission to photograph in their showroom.

Picture Acknowledgements: Beamish Open Air Museum
19 *(right)*; Bridgeman Art Library/Linley Sambourne House
21; Chris Fairclough *(cover, top left)*, 4 *(left)*, 5 *(right)*,
6 *(top)*, 6 *(bottom)*, 7 *(top)*, 7 *(bottom)*; Corbis 16-17; Eye
Ubiquitous/David Cumming 21; Hulton Getty 15 *(right)*;
Zul Mukhida 4 *(right)*, 5 *(left)*; Richard Stansfield, York
Castle Museum *(cover, centre and top right)*, *(title page)*, 8-9,
10, 11 *(top)*, 11 *(bottom)*, 12-13, 14, 15 *(left)*, 18, 19 *(left)*.

Contents

Different houses

▼ **This is a bungalow.**
It was built about 10 years ago.

▲ **This is a block of flats. It is about 30 years old.**

bungalow built years ago flats

▼ **This house was built about 80 years ago.**

▲ **This** terraced house **is more than 100 years old.
It is** Victorian.

old   terraced   house   Victorian

Roofs and windows

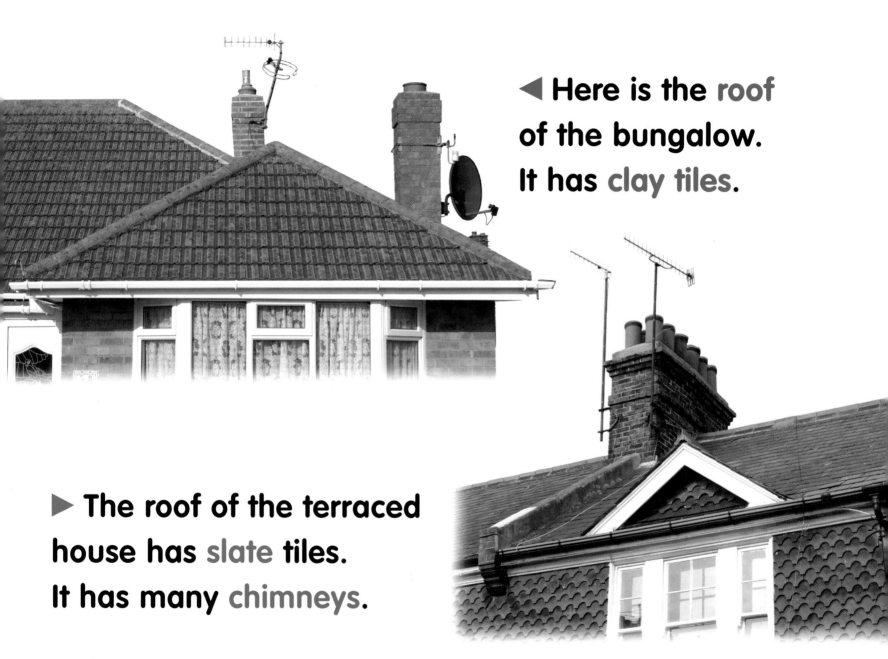

◀ Here is the roof
of the bungalow.
It has clay tiles.

▶ The roof of the terraced
house has slate tiles.
It has many chimneys.

roof clay tiles slate chimneys

◀ **The bungalow has** plastic window frames.

▶ **The terraced house has** sash **windows. How do they open? The frames are made of** wood.

plastic window frames sash wood

Inside a Victorian house

This is a living room from Victorian times.

The **mantelpiece** is over the **fireplace**. ....

What can you see on the mantelpiece?

mantelpiece   fireplace   pictures

There are many pictures on the walls.

The floor is covered with a rug. Underneath the rug are floorboards.

How is this living room different from your living room at home?

rug   floorboards   home

Fireplaces

Here is the Victorian fireplace.

The coalscuttle and tongs are next to the fire.

What are the tongs for?

coal scuttle   tongs

▲ This fire is in a house
that is 50 years old.
The fire uses electricity.

▶ This modern fire uses gas.
It looks as if it burns wood.

electricity   modern   gas   burns   11

A kitchen from the past

This is a kitchen from about 60 years ago.

How is the sink different from the sink in your kitchen?

kitchen   sink

There is a **pressure cooker** on the **stove**.

The **kettle** is also on the stove.
Many modern kitchens have electric kettles.

How else is this kitchen different from a modern one?

pressure cooker **stove** **kettle** *13*

Changing cookers

This Victorian cooker was called a 'range'.

It burned wood or coal.

Food cooked slowly in the oven beside the fire. ⋯⋯⋯

14

cooker   range   coal

◄ **This is an electric cooker from 50 years ago.**

How is it the same as a modern cooker? How is it different?

▲ **This modern microwave uses electricity. It cooks food very quickly.**

oven   microwave

A modern bathroom

▶ **This bathroom has a basin, a bath and a toilet.**

What else can you see that belongs in a bathroom?

bathroom basin bath toilet

◄ **There is a shower over the bath.**

In the past, many homes didn't have bathrooms.

People washed in a tin bathtub in the kitchen or the living room.

shower past tin bathtub **17**

Toilets inside and outside

Here is the toilet in a modern bathroom.

The seat and lid are made from plastic.

seat   lid   handle

◀ This toilet is from about 60 years ago.
It was flushed by pulling the handle on the end of the chain.

▲ One hundred years ago most toilets were like this one.
They were outside the house.

flushed   chain   outside

Which is older?

One of these bedrooms is modern and
one is Victorian. Can you tell which is which?

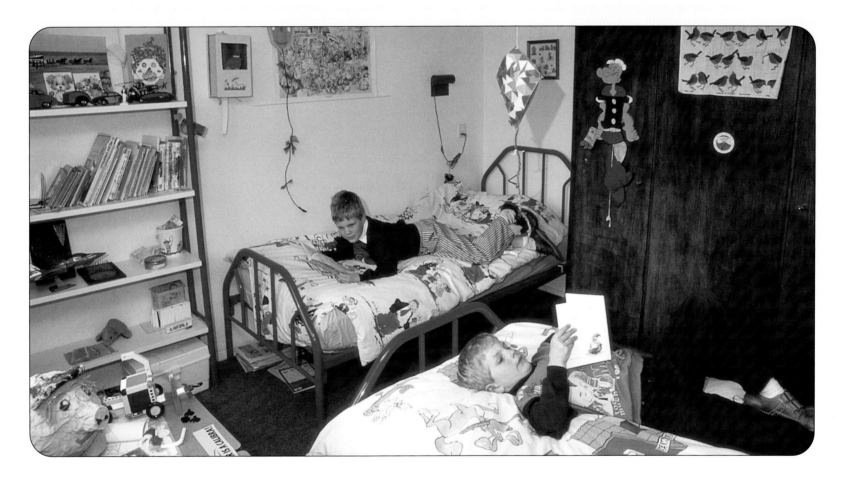

Look carefully at the beds, the furniture
and the decorations.

bedrooms   beds

The bedroom on the left is modern.
The one on the right is from Victorian times.

furniture   decorations

21

COUNTY LIBRARY

JN/2122552

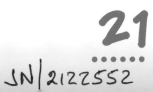

Further information for

New history and homes words highlighted in the text:

ago	clay	gas	oven	slate
basin	coal	handle	past	stove
bath	coal scuttle	home	pictures	terraced
bathroom	cooker	house	plastic	tiles
bathtub	decorations	kettle	pressure cooker	tin
bedrooms	electricity	kitchen	range	toilet
beds	fireplace	lid	roof	tongs
built	flats	mantelpiece	rug	Victorian
bungalow	floorboards	microwave	sash	window
burns	flushed	modern	seat	wood
chain	frames	old	shower	years
chimneys	furniture	outside	sink	

Background Information

CHRONOLOGY OF SELECTED BACKGROUND INFORMATION

1890s Domestic electric light in homes of the well off. Bulk of the population living in sub-standard housing without gas, electricity, bathroom or inside lavatory.

1900 First electric cookers appearing. Gas cookers widespread in wealthy homes.

1907 First electric washing machine.

1919-24 Increased subsidies for council housing.

1919-39 2.5 million private homes built. Average price of a 'semi' £450.

1935 12% population living in overcrowded conditions (two or more per room).

1936 17.8% population of York unable to afford adequate food, housing, heating and lighting.

1939 90% homes heated by open fires. 66% homes wired for electricity.

1945 70% Britain's houses pre-1914.

1947 Green belts introduced around large cities.

1948 Microwave oven invented.

1951 33% British homes without a plumbed bath.

1954 Transistor radios available.

1956 22.5% Scottish homes overcrowded.

Parents and Teachers

1960s St Anne's district of Nottingham: 91% homes with outside lavatory; 85% without bathrooms, 54% without a hot water system.

1970s Fitted carpets and use of showers (rather than baths) becoming widespread.

1980s Home ownership growing rapidly.

1990s Housing shortage owing to swiftly growing number of households.

Possible Activities:

Visit to nearby homes of different periods.

Draw features of homes from different periods.

Make a frieze timeline.

Work out how people lived from the objects that surrounded them – e.g. the amount of time needed to clean a range meant that it either stayed dirty or someone spent a long time each week cleaning it. Who?

Make a 'home corner' of different rooms and periods.

Invite adults in to talk about their homes at some specific time in the past.

Some Topics for Discussion:

Differences between homes of the same period – e.g. Victorian mansion and slum.

Role of servants before labour-saving devices.

Health and the spread of bathrooms and flushing toilets.

Safety in the home – open fires, etc.

Changing design and materials for household objects.

Further Information

BOOKS

FOR CHILDREN

Homes Discovered Through History by Karen Bryant-Mole (A & C Black, 1996)

Bedrooms by Richard Wood (Hodder Wayland, 2000)

Bathrooms by Richard Wood (Hodder Wayland, 2000)

20th Century: A Visual History by Simon Adams (Dorling Kindersley, 1996)

FOR ADULTS

Penguin Social History of Britain: British Society 1914-45 by John Stevenson (Penguin, 1984)

Penguin Social History of Britain: British Society Since 1945 by Arthur Marwick (Penguin, 1990)

Cambridge Social History of Britain, 1750-1950 by F.M.L. Thompson, (ed.), 3 Vols (Cambridge, 1990)

WEBSITES

http://www.educate.org.uk/teacher_zone/classroom/history/unit2_lesson4.htm

PLACES TO VISIT

Victoria and Albert Museum, London.

Many local museums have excellent displays and other curriculum-related material and activities, for example Southampton's Tudor House Museum.

Index